blue
Ted Walter

moon

WillingWords

Orpington, Kent
Tel : 01689 858639

Willing Words

First published in 1999 by
Willing Words
'Highfield' 29 Crown Road,
Chelsfield, Orpington, Kent
BR6 6JN
Tel : 01689 858639

ISBN: 0-9537743-1-7

Book designed by John Stibbs
Printed and bound by Typecast, East Peckham, Kent

Acknowledgements

Learning about the 'worth' of one's poem is a slow yet fascinating process, engaging as it does with editors and with the poets one comes to know well enough to ask for an opinion. My learning has been helped by the editors of The Scarpfoot Zone, The Visit, Outposts, Orbis, Envoi, The Good Society Review, Weyfarers, Agenda, Ver Poets, South East Arts Review and Pandora's Books, all of whom have accepted one or more of these poems over a period of twenty years. Several appeared in my first collection 'Choosing Yellow', published by Peter Brown of Yorick Books of Canterbury. To him I owe a great debt for getting me started.

Since then I have had equal cause to be grateful to Anne Cluysenaar, Francis Horovitz, Roger Garfitt, Jeremy Hooker, Jon Silkin, Pauline Stainer, Michael Curtis, John Rice, Dr Sheila Smith and particularly to Anne Stevenson, for fair criticism and support. Thanks are due also to those students and friends who have pointed out my strengths and weaknesses and finally to my wife who has an acute ear for over-ripe cliché.

This book is the result of such help and would not have been possible without the enthusiasm of John Stibbs, the designer, to whom many thanks.

Contents

Night Lake

Inked-in trees absorb, through gnarled bark, night.
Mute lakes among stars leaves await Autumn, still.
Heightened sound, a creak in this timbered bridge
under my lowered foot, wakes from garrisoned reeds
a dabchick's gabbling fright, choked back to silence.
I am drawn by the pull of space yet held here,
crossing close to a surface where depth is above me
and height where stars gleam cold in silken water.

Freed from gravity's weld, far-falling, my mind
from my body whispers as trees diminish, surrounding
the lake's clear eye. One blink may blind me and yet,
at home with the beasts in my past, I quench my thirst
with them; sabre-toothed tiger, wolf and tribes of men.

How many soldiers tramped from darker recesses,
rested, refreshed here? Or bodies lay as though
sleeping? Or lovers flattened long grasses
in delicate clearings? Or cattle stood in shallows?
Or fishermen cast in twilight, patient feet
at the edge imprinting clay and slow time.
On their fossil shoulders I may reach beyond stars,
beyond bright journeying probes, to the melting power.

Departure

Mud on the road and wheel-tracks show
they've gone. The grass yellow, crushed
like a marked-out building-site but now
these shapes are of things that were,
traces that will soon disappear.

This one is an arena, the outer rim
rutted, the centre littered with rubbish.
For a week no light reached here, a dim
underworld while, above, dodgem-cars crashed,
their contacts crackling, the ceiling meshed.

Here a large circle. In this sounds
the organ and bright horses ride; rising,
falling against a blur of faces. Round-
abouts for smaller children, smaller circles;
shapes for rolling pennies, shooting, candy-floss.

The grass will grow back. Even now smells
of oil and sticky sweets fade, bright lights
and excitement gone. Heavy wheels
have moved on. Some other field senses
their coming, remembers the past, flinches.

Here it is quiet. Mothers pass with shopping,
youngsters head for the slide at the far end,
the groundsman drags the huge roller, stopping
by the dipping rope that keeps us off
while, among nearby trees, rooks cough.

Ledmores, Glos

Young then we accepted trees on the ridge
as friends, climbing their branches
as into the arms of parents. Autumn
scattered under a clear sky
bronze fragments, lilting in air
that toyed with their long fall.

Downhill our hands dipped, clutched,
danced over heads, chasing leaves,
wishes loud in the light of our minds.
Caught, leaf and the wish combined
to become truth; missed, there would be time
to face uphill, watch, wait for some more.

Years spin off our lives, some caught
before touching the ground, others
missed and forgotten. Yet we
are both trees and children always;
rooted deep yet dancing, our leaf-wishes
falling, fulfilled and the unfulfilled.

The Visit

We went there once, trailing my sense
of direction so far beyond town
it thinned till it snapped. Since
then I have not been back. The return
train was a long time coming: a single
platform in the late evening light, our walk
across frightening acres to silent rails,
with a bright, particular memory
forming to last a life's time. The well.

There had been other children. 'Yes, play
in the garden but don't go near'. Words
that were bound to prompt daring. They
knew handle and rope, bucket, which boards
to be moved. A cool, cold draught
released into apple-green air and sky,
minute down there, glinted, a gift
of silver, fragmenting to slivers
of light, dripping down, the rope taut.

They wound it back up. An age shivers
through memory, poised for the first taste
and, clear on my tongue, it enlivens
the years; sharp as a stolen apple, crystal-
sweet from the rim of a cup left
at the well's edge. Clouds hung level
with distant hills. The boards we trod
at the halt gave back the day's heat,
my thirst quenched in the deepening silence.

Ornamental Pond - Waystrode Manor

Timbers, wattle and daub, mossed tiles, Tudor chimneys,
remain still. The surface moves, shivers,
responds to the faintest touch, is pulled taut,
shimmers beneath air's breath
or the skip of an insect back into sky.
Clocks on the bank, seeds snatched from time,
drift down - weightless are weighed,
the tip of a vee widening as ripples fan out
into small gongs of silence spanning the silk;
arcs interweaving, lost under low banks.

There, where reflections hang, mystery deepens.
Concentricities tap small knuckles on empty casements;
leaded lights ride in depths - fish under eaves -
as the slow crow drowns with the dove
beyond water-boatmen whose skilled craft,
the centres of circles, skate across cloud.
There is no certainty, no long comprehension,
but there at your feet is a blue infinity.

Always

Field, cloud and sunlight combine
to fill a framed space; the window
glazing a hole in air where once
no house stood. Oaks on the horizon
are older and about them are shadows;
fine patterns on soil turned by harrow
or plough, in the sweeping heads of wheat
or, deeper in time, above woods
bending beneath wind, as rain beats
where men huddle, their food raw,
lacking the hope of fire.

Movement of sun, moon, cloudscapes
that change by the hour, these are.
Timeless, the track of time over land
tells only the fall of seed, carried
on wind, the new growth, the decay
back into time's keeping. Here,
at the Weald's edge, is earth, air, sky.

Dene Hole: Farningham Wood

Fenced off, the darkest of shadows
among brambles, it dropped emptily.
Thrown stones were sucked into
a long silence then a faint clatter,
as though into the lair of a beast
crept there from stories. A mystery,
threatening from beyond split chestnut.

Now bushes have grown, trees climb
with their carved initials, the dark
mouth lost beneath dense leaves.
A weathered board, a faded warning,
and knowledge acquired with years,
remove the fear but not the mystery.

Was it the Danes digging to safety?
Who hacked at seams of flint, tallow
guttering, hauling through smoky air
minute life, turned obdurate by time
and silence, from a once ocean floor?
Forested it was home. Their clearings
are our fields, littered with skull-like
stones that, struck, create fire, light.

Sarre

Can you hear the sound of a thousand roots
holding earth together under this field?
Or is it the dull thump of boots walking
to work in every weather when there was work?
It could be the whistle and crump of shells
from across the Channel, the war half over
with people still living in fear, diving
for cover beside the shock of wheat-sheaves
on the quarter-hour after midday. Does the sound
come from under the ground: chalk being hewn,
cool larders for keeping food fresh in summer?
Or are they sounds from far centuries; commands
in foreign tongues, oars being drawn inboard,
galleys sliding against the jetty where now,
at the end of the causeway, the mill
carries rhythmically turning sails,
and the stones' long grinding rumble?

Bosham

It is easy to see now,
parked by the roadside,
slow tide rising like mercury
among grasses, silvering tarmac,
how such silent encroachment
might listen to a King's word.

Across the harbour,
shingle spire corn-coloured
among red roofs
riding at anchor,
the church contains Cnut's daughter.
Dust of an eight year old
in a stone coffin.

It is easy to see now
the King, his throne, the panoply
at the sea's edge,
his people trusting like children
from a safe distance,
his hands raised and the tide
declining to notice.

Yet here I could believe
I had the power,
tide on the turn.
No pause, no sense of achievement;
one second swilled to my feet
the next receding,
continuing to recede.

With it my heart goes out
to a King without choice;
unable to stop the tide rising
nor the life of his daughter
draining too quickly.

Looking North

Yes nurse, I know the window is over there,
with a view on to neat hedges and borders where
everything has its place, but I prefer, if
you don't mind, facing the north wall when a stiff
wind blows from the east. It is only then
I think I can hear the sea and watch coals brighten
in a remembered hearth, knowing the chimney will suck
smoke out into the night, not to be blown back
by a westerly. No. Not strange. I was born
facing north, with sea-sound from over the dunes
at the back of the house and, down Ferry Lane,
the river, an estuary, tide flowing in
from the right always. And, from over there nurse,
where yesterday's flowers wilt in their blue vase,
ships would come to the jetty, unload their catch.
Across the river was marshland, a distant church,
a lighthouse and those people who faced south.
It's in the small of my back. Even my teeth,
when I had some, knew if I used the ferry.
All day, walking there and returning, I was wary,
the wrong side of the river, happy only
once back with familiar patterns in place. Finely
drawn, not a web but a way of knowing. Home.

I guessed that when I came to leave, when time
said enough is enough, I would miss the thinly
laid shadow in north light, and not that only
but the faint blush of the rose, the contrary
honeysuckle under the eaves. All gone. Sorry.
It's not your fault. I imagine that near death
such thoughts come. It's the crossing you see, south
side to north again. And no going back. It's rich
at my age, fearing the ferryman but there's not much
I can do about it. Would they take the hearse
back through the village? Father took me across
once. Into Southwold to collect a coffin.
The lid rattled on the way back, the chain
on the ferry echoed the noise but louder; a drone
so familiar as dusk came down, with the forlorn
calling of a solitary curlew and the slack
tide sucking at timbers. They were half-sounds as I woke
with the cart rolling to firm land. I was nine,
but the south side, our side, was protection.
Perhaps, if I can pretend it is that life
I return to, the last trip won't be so bad. If
I doze off, nurse, facing the wall, you'll know where
I've gone. If you can't wake me, please leave me there.

Hospital Entrance : A21

She is thinking 'good boy' to each foot,
proud of their steps as she breathes
the scent of roses. Thorns of remembrance
prompt her forgetfulness. Where
does the pavement lead? What is the point
of her journey? The day's darkness,
adroitly obedient, covers
that girl's smile, hides the skipping child.
At night their ghosts will return,
a faint collage beside her bed,
but here trees wear smaller darknesses
and there are sneers behind bland faces.
She listens to one car's roar,
to one set of heels tapping,
to one scream of light as a window opens.

When the flower-seller offers a carnation
her twigs of words, tinder-dry,
snap with the fear of fire; consonants
threatening vowels, her tongue tied.
She is turning back, her shoulders
wrenched round by her past, turning back
knowing her feet have been called.
'Here boy. Heel.' Journey and nightfall
will merge in the nothing that sleep is.

The Baker's Daughter

'They say the owl was a baker's daughter.
Lord! we know what we are but not what we may be.'
(Hamlet)

Village dogs barking
broke the valley silence.
Into stone sunlight
he stepped from leaf-darkness,
wearing the day's heat
like a shroud.
At the half-open door,
baking bread creating a need,
he leaned a weary hand.

Alone, the baker's daughter,
fearing his grime,
the caked sweat,
his scratched forehead,
blushed her refusal;
soft, floured hands
tremulous as moths,
agitating him away.

Later,
at the far end of the village,
three men hung in the heat.
None had accused her
yet somehow the curse came.

That night perhaps,
a full moon calling,
she stretched her arms wide
pleading her fear.
Did her long gown fall,
feathered down appear
like dust from the bakery?
Was her first cry
the 'Who?' of not knowing?

It seems hard this conversion
to silent searching;
the nocturnal flight,
never able to bear
the full light of day.
But how many times
risk we the same fate
as that owl-trapped spirit?

Carols at the Crib

No gasping nor pain now, her face shone.
He, new and wondering, lay,
Air heavy with breathing. They stood,
Oxen and sheep, sheltering,
Witness to time's hold, held moment,
Their hide, fur, fleece lifting,
Hearts beating no faster, a calm chord
Charming the quiet air.
Her stare of wonder, of wordless Oh!
How can it be? Call, carol,
Shout to the hillside where men stand
Waiting to hear. See
Angels of light lift, hover, heaven-sent
Clear over the crib. Carry him
Out to the world where now we know
He is here. Here. Look.
Breathe in this new air, Christ given.
Lose your last lingering fear.

Late Thaw

Raised with excited hands the height
of stretching fingertips, tall snow,
man-shaped, stood cold.

Though pebbled eyes, shining with sun's sight,
stared, no light infiltrated
bleak isolation.

Excited dancing, feet patterning deep,
snow-mown lawn with mad perforations,
failed to move him.

Shouts and the sounds of battle, bursting
white missiles hurled through the morning,
prompted no feeling.

Laughter and scarves from November guys,
too loveable to burn, wrapped no warmth
round his cold shoulders.

His shadow lengthens, tree shade fading,
house windows beckon children
calling goodnight.

Darkness. Deep in the ice, locked atoms
remember small fingers shaping. Love
moulds a warm thought.

Cloud from the west grows darker, hiding
a crescent moon, the wind rising. Rain
splinters black pebbles.

Dumbly the day-old snowman, guarding
discarded gloves, a child's red shovel,
begins to diminish.

Memento

These tubers needed sunlight. Spreading
as they have, under the tree, their flowers
are few. Time for transplanting. Earth
falls from long roots; weeds, the small snails
disturbed with them, hauled above ground.

The `where? that hovers - a heap of potential
lying in transit - holds the grey sky
still. Flowers, tall and beautiful, tremble
over there; soil, broken by frost, empty
and waiting. Holes dug, each tuber defines tomorrow.

Iris, messenger of the gods, present in rainbows,
you of the tender nature, helper, a friend
to mortals, may you find home here, and bring
to this corner your brief, fragile beauty,
remembering this morning and the first fine rain.

Release

Past midnight. Other windows are dark,
reflecting the full moon. This one is lit.
A still flame burns, but will she come back?

The garden is grey. Shadows are black.
Seed-heads of thistledown shine, haloes of light.
All still. Will she ever come back?

Here in the room, in shadow I wait,
watching light burn. Hours shorten the wick,
black in the hollow of flame. Nights

keeping watch have held me awake
moving my eyes from flame to moon;
from stillness to slow-moving arc

and back. Tonight the flame dips. My shadow
slips across walls, skitters to corners, slides
over the floor, leaps as air flows

through the room. Her scent, stronger than when
she lived. Then, once again, calm. Outside,
lightly let go, lifts thistledown.

Full Moon - July

The moon's slow climb through heavy air
pulls a tremor in its wake;
a sense of stillness far from calm,
a boding thought before aggression,
a hint of sullen power to quell
all smiling hope. This is no moon
on which to wish nor light to heal
tired eyes. The almost angry glow
will challenge any sentiment.
On such a night there is little to be done
with sleep but welcome minutes lost
among wakeful hours. At one such waking
a fox begins its strangled bark,
rising to a cut -off scream. The sound,
entering on hot night air, chills.
Cousin to wolf, the creature barks again,
disturbs the room where shadows change
for dawn. The fox, the sense of threat
are gone when, waking next, you cancel the alarm.

Crop Circle

It is night It is summer
A small copse stands
like a childhood gang assuming nonchalance
Beneath stars a stillness
as the earth revolves
Held breath A beginning
Like the place where a hand cannot tell
very hot from very cold
Here
A frontier Air flows
Becomes soft contains power

Dissembles Thins Not warm
not cold not close not space
Cathedralled by presence
wheat stirs in the moon's light
One stalk
twists curves bends
the next next dozens
Swathes swirl lie flat
A gathering strength
Almost silent Sap in the wheat
sluicing a faint wash of sound
Old voices lost accents beseeching a welcome

Against the Light

Slowly, bearer of memory, into the low angle
of a pale sun's light, one seagull
steadily passes over the roof-tops. Still
air holds no sense of wing-beat, only
the dying light of a winter sun too ill
to climb higher. No wonder man
once feared that warmth would not return.

Later, at the back of the house,
a full moon, mistily haloed where trees
seem to hold, like reeds, the pale face,
floating, serene yet lifeless,
drifting, after the sun's loss,
to light late smoke, ash
greying a tindered memory, leaves gone.

Surely the year's end, this? No sense
of continuity for those left
in the days before understanding. Men
without temples lit fires to tempt
back the sun. What use was the moon?
Light with no warmth, full, then all too soon
dwindled to nothing; nights still-born.

Of Influence

Sometimes an early autumn light
seems to lift from silent earth
regret that knowledge comes too late.
Yet harvest on the heels of life

is not the end but simply change.
Wheat becomes the flour, the bread,
becomes the man, becomes his child;
seeds fall, the earth asleep not dead.

And when we die all we have been,
all we have ever done or said,
having made our shape, lives on,
whispers in a winnowing wind

and time ensures the earth is sown
with what we were. Ideas we held,
our grains of truth, our quick seeds thrown
at random, soon become a field.

Cow Parsley

Hollow, fluted stems
stand head and shoulders
taller than dead companions;
sap solidified
where once cloud blossomed.
Stamens, multiplied
by thousands, trap stars,
each star the product
of the pulse that drove
these plants to flower.

Here, on this bank,
static jubilation -
a frozen crowd of cheers
and joyous rocketry
that yesterday, in living green,
soared high - is fixed in time
as though the sky's clear lens
had clicked on memory.

October

The year takes on a change of tense;
low angles of the light,
a few leaves falling,
their dappled lilt
a counterpoint to commonsense.
We know the longer nights
will soon be coming
and yet, air bright

twig-still, an acorn's rapid fall
suggests new life not death,
while bracken, drawing
a mid-day breath,
hums a wing-lit madrigal
as midges from their sloth
lift; a last sunning
above cool earth.

In a Blue Moon

Glass a yet silent,
milk-bottles, poised
above concrete,
suspend my evening ritual
as tall, slow-striding Orion
gathers momentum,
hurdling rooftops.

His bright constellation
dwindles beyond shadow;
the wings of my childhood
folding, unfolding, lifting
through dewfall. Beyond
the bright orbits
of lidless-eyed birds,
their solar wings glinting,
I breathe space.

With icing on each of my senses
I glide down, out of Orion,
one late November
to a cold, red-cardinalled doorstep,
my mother beside me.

Her finger, casting,
sets my sight skimming
the sky's dark surface,
touching six symbols:
'His belt and his sword,' she says.
She winds in the line
then, pointing again,
has caught fascination.

Four stars, wide, bright locations,
thighs and his armoured shoulders.
Time-risen this giant
would welcome winter,
cold nights no longer friendless;
Orion and kinship
forged on that doorstep.

Time trails fine dust in passing,
sky-gazing less frequent,
yet, once in a blue moon,
as I welcome Orion,
the space between bottles
and concrete,
glass finally clinking,
is measured in light years.

Orion

Each minute star about my feet
is frost that from his distant voice
has travelled here. He and I meet
like this annually, the air
thinning above me, his bulk far
beyond my understanding, yet
there is a sense of deep friendship,
of arms wide open, of feet set
to take my weight were I to slip,
to make the long, slow fall up
to where he is. It is now
that the stars and the space between
can fill me, without fear. I know
their timelessness and I have been
awake beneath them walking snow,
hearing the foxes bark, watching
Orion taking his long stride
over the rope the pole star spins
and I have joined him, exalted,
atoms coursing in my blood.

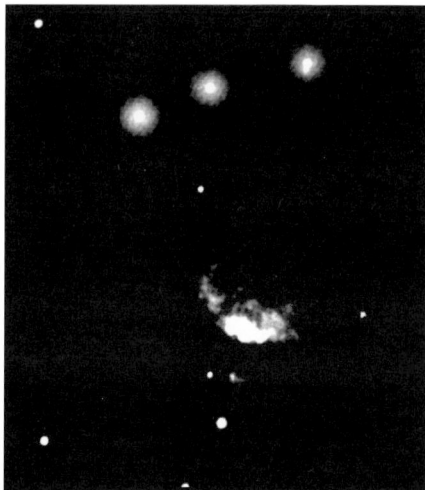

Soundings

Lines thrown, weighted, sank so far,
telling where the channels were;
voices calling, keels held clear.

Not only where but over what;
in tallow added to the weight
adhered the bits of rock or grit.

And so the lead was armed to tell
he who swung it what to call
with lives dependent on his skill.

Now signals from the distant stars
arriving here some trillion years
after they began, bring fears

of greater depths to space than Man
has found before. A black hole can
absorb a universe and then

wait for yet another one.
No arming lead to tell us when
or where we will begin again.

Universal Pastime

Sandflies on a near-deserted beach
are blown as male and female, each on each,
grapple and gesticulate, the wind
whipping them along like grains of sand.
They don't let go. The males dominate.
Though how one can distinguish male from mate
may be a chauvinistic guess. The sigh,
a satisfied or satisfying fly.

One leaves. The other takes a breath.
It's now more difficult to guess at truth.
Which one was it let the harsh wind tear
them apart and which remained? The affair
lasted seconds only, driven by a need
to secure the continuity of their breed.
The time, place and, it seems, the urge
prompting their microscopic rage,
is out of their control and yet, again,
they come in dozens just before the rain.

And time, concerned with turning rock to sand,
might find our lives more transient, less planned.

The Process

No written word holds this craftsman's spell,
for him the constant ceremony
speaks from the past to forge in ritual
an ancient metallurgy.

His lifelong repetition knows no doubt
iron and carbon will each yield
to each a subtle element and forge
a blade to cleave through any shield.

Bellowed coals are called into a white heat,
bloom on tempered metal changing,
fold on fold, billet hammered flat.
His words have a precise, anvilled meaning.

Samurai swords, thus spoken into life,
- truths of a process not set down -
are steel; a marriage where the man and wife
united through fire, wield their strength as one.

The Bridge

Beneath the bridge, in an arc of sunlight,
she beats clothes clean on a flat stone,
the stream gentle, her posture familiar;
one of patient acceptance, glad of the sun.

Above and to the right, a dark silhouette
with his back to us, he may not know
she is there. If he is aware, he ignores her,
staring upstream, overseeing his demesne.

She is kept to her work by need. Her man,
her sons expect her there. She does not fight,
watching the dirt leave cloth, clouding water.
Others, downstream, follow the same pattern.

Leaning against his fence, he flicks at his coat,
dust from the lane lying there, his pasture
lush in the sun's warmth, hay on the turn
in other fields, all his, to be passed to his son.

If her song had reached him, turning to mount,
he'd not have spoken and, if he had, disconcerted
she would have stammered an answer, curtsied.
And who, dare we say, was the more content?

Discovery

The nest is cosy, softly lined
in blind obedience some might say,
as though the constant game of chance
the birds and beasts and fishes play
had rules they kept while we, unchained,
can choose to live uncomfortably.

And yet the helix in the gene
is seen to be as purposeful
for humans as for any bird,
driving each and every cell
to imitate what is defined;
meticulous in mimicry.

So chance and choice go hand in hand,
the planned solution equally
achieved by some sublime mistake,
defying those who wish to see
man as triumphant, with his mind
the very topmost of the tree

always in charge. The bird has flown.
Some days ago, the nest still warm,
a gene said to the fledgling, "Right,
it's time you left," and from its home
it dropped, put out its wings and then
knew how good it was to fly.

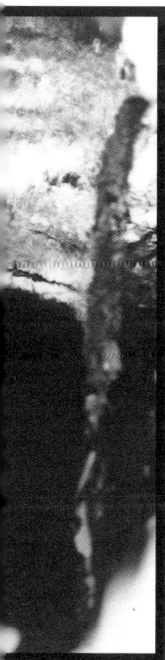

Cry Wolf

Visitors,
making ourselves at home,
discounting resentment,
we ignored, we mistrusted them;
occasional theft of sheep,
howls in the long nights,
were disturbing.

Now, after years
safe in urban homes,
a few truths claim
urgent attention,
yet we behave
as we did in the past;
loping shadows
strengthening fable.

The bad name they were given
stuck, acquired power.
Once, shouted from hillsides,
it could bring men
up from the valley.
False alarms provoked anger.
The power remains;
their mouths wired shut
to silence old fears.

But we know that their young
are obedient,
their parents loving.
Still we are wary.
We want them to be malicious.
If they have no hatred
it is our fear
that fills their howling.

The Next Assignment

The hint of a path slips under a gate
into woodland, a place of shade, secret
with unknown potential, play of light
proposing new ways, deeper insight.

There's a need to explore, examine, to lift
unturned stones, to stand quietly sifting
perceived sound, to register the waft
of luminous air tangible in leaf-drift.

Carried on light, wings scattering sparks,
minute lives, undetected in shade, speak
of the multitude, swift breaths that break
with a sigh from the universe, piercing the dark.

Needlework Box

Raining. The light is fading early.
He is bored. His toys too familiar
and it is not yet time for bed.
But the room is warm and the box
is brought downstairs. Gas-light,
popping into life, shines on veneer
and inlaid brass, worn smooth, a patina
of generations using, cleaning, tending.
It once held ..... but raise the lid.

Wooden-sided small compartments,
some lidded, the whole lifting out
revealing the secret. There is always
more space than imagined, filled
with old photographs; sepia, black and white,
tinted. Above a studio name are subjects
caught by the flare; a uniformed husband,
his mannered bride. And here on a beach,
are smiles held for that click of the Brownie.

If once the box held needles, thread,
the necessities of thrift, these photographs
she riffles through hold as much history.
Perhaps the bright bow on the hat brim
in that one was created with the box open,
the light from the oil-lamp, here, falling
on hands that later, in this one,
are wearing lace gloves, carry a parasol.
Here is one of Nellie, her sister who died.

The people and the places she mentions,
recalling her story up to this wet day,
she has named before. She will also recite
poems, once it is time for bed, remembered
from when, wearing that hat, that dress,
she went to that school. In his dreams,
her words will remain; 'The Song of the Shirt'.
`The Revenge, the 'Inchcape Rock', as well-known
as the faces, the box back upstairs again.

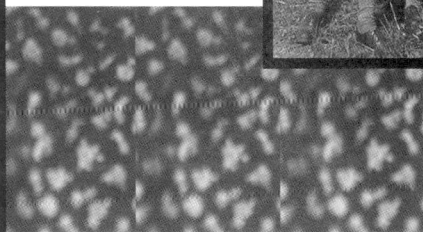

Cow and Gate

Contented sucking made the room cosy.
July, perhaps, nineteen thirty nine. Ciff,
he came to be called, was feeding. Easy
memories rose from the sound. It was as if
five summers had disappeared. The fire out,
the black range cold, the long room sunlit

and Mother smiling, the large, red tin
with the crowned baby back on the table.
Under the lid thick, sweet air, once mine,
had now stopped Ciff's crying, powder convertible
into this noise, this attention. Her lap
had been my home but then I had grown up.

With this new focus 'cowandgate' was a sound
to be shared, like 'codliveroilandmalt',
and, later, 'syrupafigs'. Even 'home'. Soon
school would teach how to read, how to write,
how to understand that 'brother' meant distance,
and how not to look for that milk-warm glance.

1939

We knew they were there,
the gaslight roaring faintly,
turned pages crackling through
warm silence like friendly lightning,
with the rush of flame from coals
settling as the evening lengthened.
With clicks too, her needles methodical,
rhythmic, as his pen softly established
a day's work. Their common togetherness
held sounds they did not hear; our lullaby.

War made it possible, the first months,
lying downstairs, tucked as suggested
in by the chimney-breast, where bricks
would withstand all but the worst.
With us supposedly sleeping
they had to be quiet; the odd word
loud, movements exaggerated.
Even a shifting of weight placed them,
chairs having their own noise.
Then of course the clock chimed
or the radio spoke its news
which they understood. Their voices
murmured concern, a counterpoint
to the bland B.B.C. Beyond our walls
a siren might wail but, blacked out,
thick curtains secure, no peeping light
betraying our presence, we knew we were safe.

Summer 1940

Knock in the nail. Watch the point
go in, the nail shorten under blows;
nail movement, thud upon thud, work.
Sit, back to the shed door, look
at the hammer, the grain of wood, the haft
polished by older hands. Light should
fall on the yard, on the path down
to the gate, the foam of suds in the drain,
and a tin bath where water, a pale blue
washed from the dipped bag, is the sea,
`boats' rocking. Look up. These leap into place
except for one stone. The low wall
has a hollow in concrete. The nail home,
drop the wood into the bath, a bomb, bursting.
The blue sky resonates, ripples tighten
into the centre, expand, overrunning
later arrivals. A milk bottle sinks,
a soap dish flounders, awash. Sounds
carry across back gardens. A bell
marks noon where nurserymen work
under glass. Water stains fade. The sheet
fills out, pulls the line taut, steam
and her song drift from the open door.

Homecoming

The back door opened into darkness
and the familiar smell that was ours.
With legs weak from sleeping in the bus
the hallway seemed long, parents gone ahead.
Gas-light chains tinkled against glass.
A match was struck. With a pop there was light.
The mantle glowed but the room was cold.
The curtains were pulled against the dark.
Shivering, the need was to be carried to bed.

Rehearsed on the return journey,
with the bus half-empty and the hour late,
each event confirmed that it was still home,
darkness always the first welcome.
Tradition enhanced that homecoming. Now switches
release known shadows at once. These rooms
are startled into being while one of us fills
the kettle. But who remembers when
this habit began? And where are the children?

Both with sons of their own now they will,
when they return, manage the keys in the back door,
tug against rain-swollen wood and, if dark,
fumble for light. Switches and rooms changed
since they were young, they will find
an age held in books and pictures. They will look
for signs of their past, beginning a new tradition
with no gaslight, no memories of the long room
that bloomed into life in their father's home.

Gauntlets

Black leather, well-worn, the cuffs wide
and gleaming, as though air still streamed
over them and the handle-bars
of his first machine, a Royal Enfield.

Gauntlets, beret and goggles, held him,
retained him though long discarded;
cracks in the leather, stains from oil,
the smell, calling through years of absence.

Riding pillion, behind his heavy black coat,
clinging .... "Grip with your knees. Lean with the bike."
Dipping into a corner, frightened at first, shifting
to remain upright. "Lean!" Shouted above engine, wind.

So gripping tight there came, with exhilaration,
praise, "He rides like part of it now". But she frowned.
The machine was taking them from her. One day it would kill:
a windshield splinter, becoming her son's singular relic,

a sharp defiance, like his refusal to cry.
Until then she would wave goodbye,
envy their maleness, feed baby,
dust the house, long for a daughter.

But she would know fear when, from sunlight,
the engine cold, beret too big,
with goggles propped on his nose, her son
stepped in, grinning, hands lost in gauntlets.

That Day

Riding the bicycle he'd let me borrow,
I slowed on the bridge over the railway
to ask the time. Below us the station
was quiet, warmth from the sun
drawing tar smells from wood, steel-sheen
silent, no train due. 'About one,' I was told,
'Maybe ten to.' I sat back on the saddle
and, wheels flicking gravel, pedalled on.

There was no hurry then, no sense of duty;
I could be home easily in time for tea.
Dad was out on his round on his Royal Enfield,
and Mum busy with whatever her Saturdays were.
In an outdated age, with almost no traffic,
I pedalled through lanes and over the hill,
alternately sunlit or ambushed by leaf-shade,
passing the white cross cut into turf.

The road I knew well, from poplars to cornfield,
welcomed me back as I rode past the school
and free-wheeled to where Lew Booker was standing,
quite near the kerb but not outside his gate,
nearer to ours as if waiting for me,
"There's been an acident, Ted. Your mother's indoors."
"It'll be O.K., Mum." I was quite certain.
"But, Ted, " I remember, "he's dead" she was saying.

Inheritance

I must show you the book. I'll get it down.
It's here with his others behind the glass.
Do you see as the door swings, the room's reflection?
It used to be like that at home. His bookcase
had tapered leaded panes and the room
would reel once he had turned the key. Then the smell,
the almost wood-smoked smell of ancient pages,
mingled with tobacco smoke, brought a sense of rest.
He'd not much of that in the late thirties, stuck
in a job he didn't like, with a wife, a child,
a motor-bike on which to do his rounds,
and often tired. We'd not to make a noise.....

These were all his. Plato, Socrates,
and this, Huxley's Lectures & Lay Sermons
given by a friend for Christmas '29.
He was nineteen and living at The Lodge then,
his parents both in service at the House,
yet he had not only read but understood these;
way beyond the reading in our neighbourhood.
It was his love of ideas and her store
of remembered poems, that made us different.
But these were sacrosanct. I was not to touch.
Nor were they opened after he was killed.
A car hit him head-on. Just thirty-nine.
And, at fifteen, I'd no time for his books.

Nor would I grieve. You see the spine in gold?
'Everyman' edition, J. M. Dent. Thousands of them
in old book shops. The paperbacks of yesteryear'
they contained, like this one, knowledge of the world,
the universe, to forge in minds ideas it seems
each age seeks to discover for itself.
But think of what it was that brought us in.
The flints we hit. Digging through sold chalk
we lifted them into light; flints never seen
in several million years, nor seen when formed,
Then you struck one with your spade. Sparks flew
and, unexpectedly, it broke open. Hollow.
Into our air ancient air gave breath,
and I recalled the first time such a flint
revealed itself. The sense of mystery
brought me indoors to write. Here's what I wrote.

Elemental motes descend
the long slow swell of time,
shell and frail skeleton
drift down through darkness;
fine dust to silt
clamped water-tight and hardening.
Each calcite death
fused to layered centuries,
compacting into chalk
while silica becomes steel-blue,
immortal memory.
Entombed a sponge
holds its hollow breath.

The rise and fall of land
brought flints to light.
Chipped into tools,
razor-sharp; an axe-head,
glinting in the light,
had, curved along the edge,
a million creatures
from primodial seas.

The sparks you made had, at their centres, darkness
burning. Life is like that. I did not grieve?
Untrue. The grief went deep, remaining there
until the poem came, for then I stepped in here
to open this book at this page, the first lecture.
'On a Piece of Chalk", dated eighteen sixty-eight.
Huxley is seeking to show that the depth
and the expanse of chalk - 'a cubic inch
of which contains hundreds of thousands
of minute bodies' - will prove the Earth's vast age.
He adds that five per cent of all the chalky mud
consists of shells and skeletons of pure flint!
My father had read this. I never had.

Death deprived me of his companionship,
but in these pages I could meet his mind.
It was as though he spoke and so absolve
me of the guilt I'd known the day he died;
that quick rush of relief. He had been stern,
you see, returning from the war, uncertain.
For we had survived without him. Given time
that might have eased but instead he died
before I could become accustomed to
his pleasure in his maturing son. This book
broke open all those years of my restraint,
releasing grief and bringing into light
awareness of our ceaseless urge to know.
Perhaps you'd like to take it with you now?

Distances

Go on, run ahead, the air tense
with excitement. A game.
Dare to leave, hand warm,
waving until she waves.
Or hang back, stop, let her walk on,
watch her grow small.
Either way run.
Totter into arms that, lifting,
swing up, spin, put young feet back down.

The game is preparation; a tram
clanking away with her,
London a seething hum,
legs crossing the lines feet tread,
not knowing the secret. She will return
stepping each centre cleanly
as she taught. Wait,
laugh when you see her run;
her tears, her praise, unexpected.

Now time is distance,
her face and her shape vague
since she made the last journey,
but there persists the sense
of waiting.... of running.

Jig-saw

A cold day, one for talking before the fire, but the warmth
between us not flames, speech;
her words coming alive at last, the lid
off the box, pieces jumbled together, a few joined;
proof she had started before, then given up.

It had required care, delicate tact,
to bring them to light; to shake off
thin traces of pain, sort memories, turn
past fragments face up as, half burned,
coals settled, pieces beginning to fit.

Years later, with my life comfortably boxed,
she had torn off the lid. 'I'm dying
aren't I?' Her wide-awake eyes
jolted me back to my birth, forward
through childhood, the years spent with her.

And now, her box under shovelled earth,
the puzzle, shaken by dismembering hands,
is not complete. There are pieces missing.
Our task had barely begun yet even then
she had stared into shadows, searching.

Proof of Identity

1. Sevenoaks

Coming back here to work
is like living an old film.
Changing light across Knole
flickers among close-set trees
and the camouflaged ghosts
of waiting army vehicles
once glimpsed from a bus.

Memory has been editing,
cutting, Otford, St.Johns, gone:
the cross above Shoreham
and those armoured cars
brought closer together,
linked by the sense of war
and remembered dead.

A quick cut in between,
shows alleys behind the town,
the Buckhurst terrace
where my father's Aunt
offers scones with butter
as thin as the air
on black-japanned horses,
riders jousting in dustlessness.

Walking these roads
that drop from the town
I enter the frame
my parents lived.

63

2. Shoreham

He loving her
and her crazy gaiety;
she loving him
and his warmth of words;
both loving hills,
shadows among close beech;
I was conceived here.

3. Swanley

Council house gardens,
each a small-holding,
neighbours prodigal with plants.
In back porch shops
spuds, chrysants, onions,
and tiny sharp apples
in teeth-locking toffee,
all sold for pennies.
On warm steps, our backs
to lav doors, we swapped
comics, dogeared and readthin,
mimicking barter
while voices called over fences,
gardens away from each other.
Everyone listened but
about our backyard
golden-rod guarded a silence.

4. Riverhill

The Lodge, my father's home,
still there. Warm grey stone,
tall Tudor chimneys,
low eaves.
Behind that small window
was once my bedroom,
the sill, curtained at Christmas,
hiding the thrill of gifts.

I've just been back.
Stepping under a low lintel
into the pungency of snuffed lamps,
an oiled warmth closing about me,
doors latching open
with clicks that wake the dead.
He knew my father.
Deep in his eyes light flickers
reviewing years. He smiles.
The film re-run, my face fits.
I have come home.

Wednesday Butterfly

Here the calm sea argues an ease
that is unreal. The bright focus
on wings closed in prayer, open
in praise for the man that he was,
is through three words, 'Lew Booker's dead.'
The grasses beyond are bowing
as though to a passing entourage.

Through the eyes on the wings, years
unwind. The window-sill glares with light
searching the sky, the crack of the ack-ack
gun imminent, the last bomb close, the door
of the shelter dislodged, a mouthful of dirt
for Gran. Then, with the light of his masked torch,
his voice comes, low and caring.

In the braced legs of the insect, his shape
planting flowers; face and arms darkened
by weather and work, his chrysants
cut for market, their boxes our hideout,
war games across two back-yards. The news
of his death coming to this house, this peace,
brings with it these plentiful butterflies.

Richard

A thrown ball, a sudden gust of wind
and down fall blossom petals round his feet.
He stops his dance, laughter in his mind,
to stare at silences that seem to meet
as friends might after a long absence.
I shake a bough the more to please him
feeling, though, a traitor to the tree
that has enchanted us this spring, each limb
burgeoning in warm, still air, a complicity
with daffodils to make their entrance
unmistakeable. Both are dying now, the flowers'
twisted shapes are sloughed skins, a metamorphosis
like the one he names as petals drift. 'But-ter
flies,' he carefully exclaims. Hands lift
and, almost two, he continues in his dance.

Oliver

Enclosed lawn, clothes-horse, blanket;
his house. In its shadow a stool,
trivet and an old frying pan. Holding
two fingers he leads me there,
invites me in. My head and shoulders
share his space. He stirs earth,
offers some. 'Dinner,' he says.

He has been walking for a while now,
long enough to say 'go walk', to wait
impatiently for reins, to take
me out into his world, to touch
known walls, garden gates,
cracks in paving, small puddles.
Today we find reflected cloud.

David

"I can help," and, five years old,
hauling a stool to the sink, climbing
under and between my arms, he takes gloves
and brush and begins washing up.
Careful, casually meticulous, he
hands plates to rinse, glasses held
safely, spoons dredged from drowning
beneath suds. Lastly he loves
lifting the tea-pot, his mouth to the lip
of the spout, blowing bubbles that pop.

Reflected in multiple curves, running
with rainbows, windows shimmer
minutely and, bubble on bubble, years
burst to reveal a window, bowl,
my hands chasing foam,
lost in the delicate kissing of tiny explosions;
the milk bottle, always last, a reluctant swimmer,
gurgling down, large bubbles rising,
stars held in suspension. Here, his shared smile
holds all the help we need to be real.

Draughts

"We'll play my way." "That means I lose,"
I thought. At five he had the skill
to know how far he could insist. "Choose
your colour, I'll be red," his smile
knowing that I knew I had no chance.

The game began. He moved each piece
just where he liked and in one jump
took three of mine. I thought, "What price
rules?" "Your go Grandad." With the prompt
I made to take a red. "You can't,"

my Grandson quickly said. "Why not?"
"The rules," he said. "My rules. But leave
yours there. I won't take you." I thought,
"Oh, no?" He did and, with a suave
wave of the hand, two more beside.

"That's cheating," I rebuked, but hid
the faint frustration which began
to rise, knowing that he had not lied
but rather tested truth.
The fun was that of using words to fox

the adult world. His friendly hoax
gave him control, the chance to show
that he could work things out and next
pretend a different world. "My go,"
I said and, jumping backward, took two Kings.

Index of photographs

Page

Those images marked* are from the Needlework Box
see p 48/49. The remainder are from photos by
Ted Walter.